CONNECT

THINKING BIBLICALLY ABOUT

BEAUTY....

JAC BULL

CONNECT: THINKING BIBLICALLY ABOUT BEAUTY

Copyright © Jacqueline Bull 2007
First published 2007
ISBN 978 1 84427 271 6

Scripture Union, 207–209 Queensway, Bletchley, MK2 2EB, England
Email: info@scriptureunion.org.uk
Website: www.scriptureunion.org.uk

Scripture Union Australia
Locked Bag 2, Central Coast Business Centre, NSW 2252
Website: www.scriptureunion.org.au

Scripture Union USA
PO Box 987, Valley Forge, PA 19482
Website: www.scriptureunion.org

The right of Jacqueline Bull to be identified as author of this work has been asserted by her in
accordance with the Copyright, Designs and Patents Act 1988.

Scripture quotations taken from THE HOLY BIBLE, TODAY'S NEW INTERNATIONAL
VERSION, (TNIV). Copyright © 2004 by International Bible Society. Used by permission of
Hodder & Stoughton Publishers, a division of Hodder Headline Ltd. All rights reserved.
"TNIV" is a registered trademark of International Bible Society.

British Library Cataloguing-in-Publication Data.

A catalogue record of this book is available from the British Library.

Printed and bound in Great Britain by Henry Ling Ltd, Dorchester, England.

Cover and internal design by ie Design of Birmingham, UK
Typesetting by Carsten Lorenz

Scripture Union is an international Christian charity working with churches in more th
130 countries providing resources to bring the good news about Jesus Christ to children, you
people and families – and to encourage them to develop spiritually through the Bible and
prayer.

As well as our network of volunteers, staff and associates who run holidays, church-based
events and school Christian groups, we produce a wide range of publications and support th
who use our resources through training programmes.

CONNECT

John Stott, a former president of Scripture Union, has stressed the need for Christians to 'relate the ancient Word to the modern world.' His vision is for integrated Christians – those who have brought every area of their lives under the lordship of Christ – to penetrate the world. To this end we hope that each booklet in the Connect series will 'do what it says on the tin' – help readers think *biblically* about the big issues of the day. And, having begun to think biblically about those issues, we pray that readers will feel able to thoughtfully penetrate the world, making a biblical perspective part of their everyday conversations about those issues and part of their own everyday living.

Nigel Hopper
Matt Campbell
Series Editors

CONTENTS

INTRODUCTION

I'm about five feet two inches tall and weigh around nine-and-a-half stone. I'm wonderfully curvaceous – some would say drop dead gorgeous! My face lights up when I smile, my baby blues sparkle and I have hair every bit as glossy as a 'because you're worth it' ad. In short, I'm beautiful. Just ask anyone who knows me; anyone who laughs with me when I crack another corny joke; anyone who cries with me when I feel like a bad mother; anyone who shares my life. They think I'm beautiful. But they're not blind. They are, of course, aware that I'm (some would say) a little short and towards the top end of my ideal weight with a well-rounded figure. They can see crooked teeth when I smile and bags beneath my eyes. They witness my bad hair days. They know and I know that I'm no Kate Moss, Victoria Beckham, Keira Knightley or anyone else but me. And still, curiously, they would undoubtedly tell you that I am beautiful.

Perhaps it's like that for you, too? You know that you miss the mark – if that mark is perfection – but nonetheless you think you're a pretty impressive specimen, and so do those around you. Of course, if you were going to go down the route of comparing yourself to others at work, at college, on the TV or in magazines, you might feel a bit rubbish, a bit inferior ... but it's generally best not to go there. Unfortunately, there are influences around us and, I suspect, even in us, that end up making us go 'there' quite a lot of the time. It can be pretty difficult to escape comparisons, insecurity and even a little jealousy when we're being continuously bombarded by images of physical perfection. Well, the images are *someone's* idea of physical perfection.

Of course, you don't have to be a genius, a Persian princess or a Mongolian nomad to know that beauty means different things to different people. In some cultures, the role of women as mothers can be seen as so central that to be a big woman is to be a beautiful woman, embodying the ideal of health, fertility and maternalism so valued by the society.

Or, for a totally different perspective, take the young women of the Ethiopian Hamar tribe. At tribal initiation ceremonies where the young men of the tribe leap across the backs of cattle to show their worth, these girls gather round to volunteer themselves for ritualised whippings. They do this to show their support for their brothers or cousins and to demonstrate their own courage. The scars left on their bodies are considered beautiful because of what they mean.

So, obviously, what we mean by 'beauty' can vary enormously from culture to culture. Thanks to the work of anthropologists, we know a great deal about different cultural expressions of beauty and the ideologies that lie behind them. But this isn't meant to be an investigation into anthropology – what about *theology*? Could that shed any light on our understanding of beauty? And what about the Bible, supposedly the source of Christian theology? What does it mean to think biblically about beauty?

And what about the Bible, supposedly the source of Christian theology? What does it mean to think biblically about beauty?

As we start to wrestle with these issues, don't make the mistake of thinking that this is just a booklet for women, just because the cases I've mentioned so far mainly relate to women. Beauty, the body and identity are issues which affect us all – colouring our relationships with each other, ourselves and God. So this is a booklet for anyone with a body – men *and* women.

1 BEAUTY IN THE BIBLE

It used to be regarded as only an extended metaphor for the unique love between God and his people, but now, finally, most scholars would admit that the biblical book Song of Songs is what it seems most obviously to be – a highly colourful celebration of love, in which physical attraction plays an extremely large part. Reading Song of Songs, you can't miss the earthy and exuberant celebration of physical beauty. For example, we're told in chapter 4 of the book that 'the beloved' is so beautiful that her hair is like a 'flock of goats descending from the hills of Gilead'! Her lips are like a 'scarlet ribbon' and her temples like 'the halves of a pomegranate'! There's more of course, but we can leave her 'twin fawns' browsing among the lilies for now! Even though these particular metaphors don't resonate readily with us today, we know what they mean! The experience of finding beauty in ourselves and in others has always been part of being human, and it's certainly not excluded from the Bible. Maybe this explains why, when a handsome man or a beautiful woman emerged in the story of God's people, the biblical writers thought it was worth mentioning?

The experience of finding beauty in ourselves and in others has always been part of being human, and it's certainly not excluded from the Bible.

Or we could look at what happens as the Hebrew forefathers emerge midway through Genesis and their various wives and concubines are introduced into the story. Not all of them were high-profile beauties – not enough to warrant a mention in the narrative, anyway But three women are singled out: Sarah (first mentioned in Genesis 12), Rebekah (introduced in Genesis 24) and Rachel (who turns up in Genesis 29). Now, although we don't know exactly what they looked like, we know that foreign kings and Hebrew men alike were struck by their appearance. For example, Rachel is clearly set apart from her sister, Leah, on the basis of her good looks. Even so, as Herbert Lockyer points out, Leah's ability to 'clutch and strive desperately to hold on to [her] man…' was just as strong as that of her sister. Both, he says, apparently felt that life owed them 'romance and happiness'. As their part in the story unfolds (and it's got all the ingredients of a good soap opera), the struggles of Leah and Rachel from Paddan Aram begin to seem not so far removed from the struggles of Leah from Stoke-on-Trent and Rachel from Hull today. Should Leah be singled out for her 'weak eyes'? Does Rachel's beauty make it easier for her to hold on to her man?

Should Leah be singled out for her 'weak eyes'? Does Rachel's beauty make it easier for her to hold on to her man?

Moving on beyond the patriarchs, two other significant women are singled out for their looks – Abigail (who comes into the life of David in 1 Samuel 25) and Esther (who obviously has a book to herself). And where did their beauty get them? All the way to the top, that's where! Well, being beautiful certainly *helped*, but if it hadn't been for Abigail's quick thinking and intervention, her beautiful body would have been a dead body, had David gone through with his plan to slaughter her husband's household. So she was beautiful *and* smart. In the same way, Esther was beautiful *and* courageous. Her beauty got her noticed by the Persian King Xerxes, who ruled over 127 provinces stretching from India to Cush. Sounds impressive, but anyone with a taste for facials and spa treatments would be even more impressed to learn that before a girl could be presented to the king as a potential wife, she had to undergo an epic 12 months of beauty treatments – six months with oil of myrrh and six with perfumes and cosmetics, to be precise (Esther 2)! Makeover complete and job done, it must have been tempting for Esther to conceal her identity as a Jewess, but she dared to risk her own life for the sake of her people (Esther 7).

So that's a very brief overview of some of the women

given star treatment in the Old Testament. But what about the men? Were there any Brad Pitts, Johnny Depps or George Clooneys in Israel? Well, we know that Saul was 'as handsome a young man as could be found anywhere in Israel, and he was a head taller than anyone else' (1 Samuel 9:2). We also read that David was 'glowing with health and had a fine appearance and handsome features' (1 Samuel 16:12). David's son Absalom took after his father, it seems, for 'in all Israel there was not a man so highly praised for his handsome appearance as Absalom. From the top of his head to the sole of his foot there was no blemish in him' (2 Samuel 14:25).

So, the Old Testament writers, at least, have no objection to going out of their way to note that some people were better looking than others. (The New Testament is a little more coy on the subject, with the possible exception of Matthew 14:6 – although other, more general, references do appear, which we'll pick up on later.) But whose definition of beauty are they working to? As modern Western readers of the Bible we come to the text with certain presuppositions about what beauty looks like. Given the vast gulf between Old Testament culture and our own, might we not be in for a shock if we were to discover what Sarah, Rebekah, Rachel, Saul, David or Absalom actually looked like?

And why do the biblical writers make reference at all to anyone's physical appearance? Is it always because it's essential to whatever point is intended to be made by the ongoing biblical story, or is it just a statement of 'fact', as perceived in that particular culture?

And why do the biblical writers make reference at all to anyone's physical appearance? Is it always because it's essential to whatever point is intended to be made by the ongoing biblical story, or is it just a statement of 'fact', as perceived in that particular culture? Should we take an interest in these references or just note that whilst such things may have been important at the time, they're not really relevant to us now? What is the significance of references to physical beauty in the Word of God?

Beauty and image are still very much part of our story today. Since taking over as Conservative Party leader in December 2005, David Cameron has frequently been accused of being someone who is more

But in a world where the medium is arguably the message, can anyone afford not to be concerned with image and style, including Christians?

concerned with image than with substance. But in a world where the medium is arguably the message, can anyone afford not to be concerned with image and style, including Christians? Cameron and other political leaders and celebrities of our age might make us think that our need for a 'beauty fix', to somehow enliven our lives with the glamour and excitement of the 'beautiful people', is a relatively new, media-driven fad. Maybe, though, some of the passages we've referred to suggest that it's as old as the Bible itself?

2 FIXING BEAUTY

Let's take another look at Sarah, one of the 'beautiful people' of the Old Testament. Most people, when informed of her beauty, probably instantly imagine her as *young*: perhaps in her late teens or early twenties. Maybe she had Madonna's luck, and made it in to her forties with style. But certainly by her 60th birthday, her looks may have been waning. And, surely, by the time she made it to 126 (a year before she died, according to Genesis 23:1,2), she must have looked old?

Whether we like it or not, God has given us bodies for the journey of life – and those bodies age. Realising that can be unsettling and upsetting. What do we do when our bodies look old and out of place in a world where wrinkles are a no-no? What do we do when the skin we are in is no longer celebrated – when, to borrow again from Song of Songs, the goats leave Mount Gilead and our lips look more like dried-out autumn leaves than scarlet ribbons? And as for the twin fawns… Are our bodies just packaging, like mortal jiffy bags that we are free to tamper with – a nip here, a tuck there – or is our relationship with our body more complex than that?

Every year in the UK, the beauty industry makes 8.9 billion pounds and there are 65,000 cosmetic operations. A large part of this profit and surgical activity is based on the desire to stay young-looking. And why not – where's the harm in the appearance of youthfulness?

Barbie is one of the best-selling toys of all time. She resolutely refuses to age. So could she be at least partly responsible for the rising popularity of cosmetic surgery? Even ten years ago, the plastic surgeon Maja

Ruetschi could say, in an interview with *Cosmopolitan* magazine, 'We can make better breasts than God. Women grow up with a Barbie doll – her long legs, tiny waist and huge breasts – it's no wonder they want to look like that' (*Cosmopolitan*, August 1996). Things don't seem to have changed much since then – a flick through the back pages of any issue of the same magazine today will throw up a slew of adverts offering women the chance to modify themselves to their hearts' desire. What's more, Ruetschi's passing reference to God surely brings the issue of cosmetic surgery into sharp focus for Christians. Is it an expression of both dissatisfaction with the way God has made us and of a belief that we can do better than him? Or is it just an extreme form of make-up? Then again, if corrective surgery, say after a car crash, is OK, why not cosmetic surgery? Aren't both about looking the best we can?

... if corrective surgery, say after a car crash, is OK, why not cosmetic surgery? Aren't both about looking the best we can?

CASE STUDY

You have been best friends with Daniel since Primary school. He doesn't share your Christian beliefs, but you know each other well. In fact you know him so well, share so much in common and have such a laugh together that it's difficult to believe that he's actually acutely shy. He finds it extremely difficult to talk to people, especially women. Having taken a year out after his A levels, Daniel is now planning for university next year. He has been working hard and saving money, which, he confides in you, is partly to pay his way through university, and partly to pay for plastic surgery. He desperately wants a nose job, which he believes will give him the confidence he lacks. He wants to fit in at university. He wants to feel that he is attractive.

You are shocked by Daniel's plans. He doesn't have a particularly large nose. He is, in your opinion, a good-looking bloke who simply lacks self-confidence. But Daniel is adamant that surgery is what he needs. He genuinely feels that if he can change his face, he will be happier and more confident. To what extent is Daniel thinking biblically about beauty?

3 CLOTHED IN BEAUTY

From Adam and Eve to Giorgio Armani – who would've thought that the fig leaf could inspire so much creativity? There are numerous references in the Bible to make-up, jewellery and clothing (for a brief sample, try Exodus 32:2; Numbers 31:50; 2 Samuel 13:18,19; 2 Kings 9:30; Matthew 11:8; Luke 7:25; James 2:2). At times the references are merely a passing comment in the context of something else. For example, in Jeremiah 4:30, God says to his people:

'What are you doing you devastated one?
Why dress yourself in scarlet
And put on jewels of gold?
Why colour your eyes with paint?
You adorn yourself in vain.
Your lovers despise you;
they seek your life.'

... is it a legitimate use of the Bible to infer from this passage that Christians should avoid concerning themselves with fashion and beauty because such things lose their significance when we are faced with judgement from God, or the return of Christ?

The wider context of these particular references to fashion and beauty (which are probably meant as a metaphor for all the different things that the people of Judah do to distract themselves from the service of God) is that of God's impending judgement on his people. It is not that fine clothing is condemned in itself; it is that the coming judgement makes it pointless. So, is it a legitimate use of the Bible to infer from this passage that Christians should avoid concerning themselves with fashion and beauty because such things lose their significance when we are faced with judgement from God, or the return of Christ?

At other times, however, the references seem to be a direct challenge to specific practices of decoration. For example, in Genesis 35:2, Jacob tells his household to 'Get rid of the foreign gods you have with you, and purify yourselves and change your clothes.' The passage then goes on to state that Jacob's household handed over their foreign gods and the rings in their ears. It may have been that the clothes and the rings they wore – probably as amulets or charms – were bound up with a pagan religion. In any case, Jacob's family are instructed to change their clothing in an act of purification. God apparently wanted his people to *visually* distinguish themselves from the people around them as a sign of their allegiance to him. Is it possible then that Christians should show their allegiance to Christ not only by what they do and say but also by what they wear or don't wear? After all, doesn't what we wear say something about who we are and what we are about? Christians have come up with all kinds of attempts to signal their faith like this – crucifixes, rosary beads, WWJD wristbands, fish lapel badges, slogan-heavy T-shirts, morally-motivated dresscodes – the list goes on… Should we seek to make such obvious statements about who it is we worship, and reject anything that seems to belong to 'the world' (whatever that means)? Or is even the mildest leaning towards a Christian 'dresscode' dangerously cultish and rejecting a natural right to express our own tastes and God-given creativity?

Is it possible then that Christians should show their allegiance to Christ not only by what they do and say but also by what they wear or don't wear?

The writer of 1 Peter (who is probably the apostle Peter himself) has some thoughts to throw in to the debate – thoughts which may sound slightly unfashionable (or worse) to us now! In 1 Peter 3:1–6 he addresses wives in the Christian community. Urging them to submit to their husbands he says, 'Your beauty should not come from outward adornment, such as elaborate hairstyles and the wearing of gold jewellery and fine clothes. Rather, it should be that of your inner self, the unfading beauty of a gentle and quiet spirit, which is of great worth in God's sight' (vs 3,4). Talk of shunning fine clothes in favour of submitting to husbands could sound crazy in a culture where young people frequently shun marriage in favour of fine clothes and a disposable income! The original context seems to be part of an emphasis on the winning over of non-Christian husbands who might not be convinced by preaching alone. Peter seems to think there is a beauty of character that is more important than a beautiful appearance. But does that necessarily mean he is asking Christian wives to positively shun fashion and beauty in favour of holiness? Or does this passage allow for beautiful, fashionable wives who are also beautiful on the inside?

Paul, in his first letter to Timothy, is more explicit. Speaking about how things should be when Christians come to worship he says, 'I also want women to dress modestly, with decency and propriety, adorning themselves, not with elaborate hairstyles or gold or pearls or expensive clothes, but with good deeds, appropriate for women who worship God' (1 Timothy 2:9,10). Does this mean that certain fashion statements or ways of wearing clothes are off-limits for Christians? Should Christians be using their clothing to somehow distance themselves from the culture around them in a way similar to those Muslim women who continue to wear the full-length *burka* covering on account of their religiously-motivated desire for modesty and propriety? And given the growing interest of men in beauty and fashion (even if they refuse to admit it), what are the practical implications of Peter and Paul's words for men in church? Or are their words simply of no relevance to twenty-first-century Christians, living in a vastly different culture?

Should Christians be using their clothing to somehow distance themselves from the culture around them in a way similar to those Muslim women who continue to wear the full-length burka covering on account of their religiously-motivated desire for modesty and propriety?

CASE STUDY

Sheila is 58 years old and has been a part of your church community for years. She is very involved with the children's work in the church. She has seen many children, including her own, go through the different youth groups into adulthood. She approaches you, the church youth leader, with concerns about how the young people are dressing. 'The girls expose too much flesh and the boys wear their baggy jeans halfway down their backsides, exposing their underpants! They seem to be so concerned with how they look … and the fashions today are quite indecent. I don't know what the Lord must think', she shudders. She then demands to know what you're going to do about the situation. How do you respond to Sheila biblically?

How do you respond to Sheila biblically?

ANOTHER CASE STUDY

Eva is 15 years old and has been part of the same church as Sheila all her life. In fact, she knows Sheila quite well from when she was in the group for 8 to 10 year-olds. Lately, she and others from the youth group have been feeling judged by the older people in the church. They know they are being watched and suspect that they are being talked about. To some extent they find it quite funny, and sometimes even deliberately provoke reactions in the older people, for a laugh. But the day after Sheila has spoken with you, Eva also approaches you, as her youth leader, moaning that the older members of the church look down on them because of how they dress. 'It's like they judge us because of what we look like. But that's not very Christian, is it? Anyway, they can't talk, because they don't even care what they look like. They "let themselves go" and think that's OK. Well, my God likes beautiful things and creativity, I mean, he's the Creator right?' How do you respond biblically to Eva?

How do you respond biblically to Eva?

4 HEALTH AND BEAUTY

You only have to have one ear open to hear people frequently commenting on their bodies – specifically the size, shape and weight of their bodies. It's probably women you hear talking about their bodies more than men. That doesn't necessarily mean that men aren't body-conscious, just that they feel less inclined or less able to talk about these issues amongst themselves. Men appear to be more comfortable with their bodies than women, and almost certainly feel less pressure to be thin. On the other hand, is being underweight perhaps more of a problem to men, who feel that they should look big and powerful with well-defined muscles and perfectly toned bodies?

But if our bodies are 'temples of the Holy Spirit' as Paul suggests (1 Corinthians 6:19,20), isn't it right – Christian, even – that we should be actively caring for our bodies? Yet again, if we answer 'yes' to that question, are we implying that the ideal church has room only for people who are healthy, fit and thin or actively on the way there?

... if we answer 'yes' to that question, are we implying that the ideal church has room only for people who are healthy, fit and thin or actively on the way there?

The issue becomes more complex when you realise that the desire to be thin can itself become a threat to health. Is it healthy that 75 per cent of women and 80 per cent of American 10 year-old girls diet? (Source: www.about-face.org)

The beauty product company Dove have been running an ongoing campaign to raise awareness on body image and self-esteem throughout 2006 called 'The Campaign for Real Beauty'. In its attempt to both promote the company and their products at the same time as raising unease with some aspects of the beauty industry, it's similar to another campaign promoted by The Body Shop ten years ago. One aspect of the Dove campaign was a global survey into how women feel about themselves in relation to their bodies and their physical appearance. They reported that two-thirds of women surveyed (aged between 15 and 60 years old) avoided the basic activities of life because they felt bad about the way they looked. If this is an accurate picture of the world we are living in, where is the free and full life Christians claim that Christ is offering the world (John 10:10)?

If this is an accurate picture of the world we are living in, where is the free and full life Christians claim that Christ is offering the world (John 10:10)?

The rise in eating disorders amongst young women and girls, desperate to keep their bodies a certain size and shape, has recently sparked debate in the fashion world. There is now real concern that underweight models are having a negative impact on women's body image. In August 2006 an underweight model collapsed and died after a catwalk show, having reportedly eaten nothing but leafy vegetables for months in an attempt to lose more weight. Subsequently Madrid fashion week decided, in response to pressure from local government, to ban models with a body mass index (BMI) of less than 18. (BMI is a calculation based on height and weight – UN health experts advise a BMI of between 18 and 25.) Milan fashion week followed suit, opening with a plus-size show. They also announced that they would be introducing a new code of conduct requiring models to have a signed health certificate.

Where, biblically speaking, should we draw the line between health and beauty?

Where, biblically speaking, should we draw the line between health and beauty? Should Christians be raising concerns when images of women or men are unhealthy? And to what extent must we take responsibility for the more negative side of the fashion industry – have we as consumers bought into a cultural beauty package that requires people, particularly women, to look a certain way?

The model Erin O' Connor is tall, thin and striking-looking, with angular features – not a 'conventional beauty' by any means. She says, 'My teenage years were ridiculous. I desperately wanted a boob job, I desperately wanted a nose job, I constantly had sore feet because I would buy shoes two sizes too small because I couldn't bear to buy my big shoes. I had no perception of how a woman was meant to be and how she was entitled to go with what her version of whatever being a woman was. It was only in my late teens and early twenties when I started modelling, that I began to appreciate myself' (interviewed in the *Guardian*, 21 September 2006).

So here the fashion for thin, flat-chested women is being presented as liberating, allowing Erin O'Connor to 'celebrate' her body in a way that she hadn't been able to growing up in a culture where it was curves that were the desirable body-shape. Her story presents us with an interesting possibility – maybe it's not fat or thin that's the issue. Maybe the issue is our willingness to accept and celebrate the different bodies we've been blessed with. Can't healthy thin bodies and healthy voluptuous bodies both be celebrated as beautiful? Isn't that what the Creator would have wanted?

Can't healthy thin bodies and healthy voluptuous bodies both be celebrated as beautiful? Isn't that what the Creator would have wanted?

5 INNER BEAUTY

It has been estimated that we are bombarded with between four hundred and six hundred advertisements day, of which one in eleven has a direct message abou beauty – and that isn't counting the indirect messages (source: www.about-face.org). Or flip through a coup of popular men's or women's magazines like *GQ*, *Men's Health*, *Red*, *Elle* or *Marie Claire* and you won't have to look very hard to pick up on some of the messages of both kinds. What we are to make of these images, and their effect on us, is less clear. Are they invit ing us to enter an alternative reality in which everyon is perfect and no one grows old (and we're not talking about the kingdom of God)? The *manufactured* nature of this 'other reality' disturbs many people. Surely there is a cruel aspect to the way in which elaborate make-up and photographic treatments (not to mentio computer manipulation) are used to dangle a standar of unattainable beauty before the general public?

Others might answer that there is an overlooked posi tive aspect to all of this – that such images work to show us 'ordinary' people what our own potential fo beauty is, and provide us with a spur and inspiration to help us aspire to look and feel our best. One of the advocates of this view is the US model agent Eileen Ford. She says, 'Models do not have a negative impac on women. They have a positive impact because they set standards. Women are going to look like them- selves. But they will look like their best selves becaus models set standards. When you think and feel your best there's an aura around you of self-confidence an self-assurance. Models do that to women.' A Chris- tianised version of this argument might be to say that if God is Creator and we are made in his image, then our appreciation of what's beautiful and our desire

Models do not have a negative impact on women. They have a positive impact because they set standards.

to achieve it for ourselves is God-given, and totally natural.

Eileen Ford certainly isn't the only person to connect outer beauty with inner harmony. Love them or loathe them, there's no doubting that the TV series *What Not To Wear*, accompanied by an inevitable host of copycat shows, has largely transformed the confidence and character of those who have volunteered themselves to have the contents of their wardrobes made-over. Those who fear the negative side of this part of modern culture would also say that we can see some kind of link between outer beauty and inner character. Dr Dee Dawson, a specialist in eating disorders, believes that most young anorexic girls associate body shape with glamour and success because 'Judgement of character is increasingly based on superficial appearance. We objectify celebrities, inferring all sorts of things from their physical appearance. Image colours everything, simply because, in a world overloaded with information, we cling to what is most obvious: and that's how things look.'

'Judgement of character is increasingly based on superficial appearance.'

Again, a biblical perspective would suggest that this is nothing new. When the prophet Samuel went to Jesse's house to anoint Saul's successor as Israel's king, he had to be rebuked for initially basing his assumptions on 'how things look' (1 Samuel 16:1–6). With Jesse's son, Eliab, before him, God's message was, 'Do not consider his appearance or his height, for I have rejected him. The Lord does not look at the things human beings look at. People look at the outward appearance, but the Lord looks at the heart' (1 Samuel 16:7). Given that we are advised by Paul to 'Follow God's example … as dearly loved children' (Ephesians 5:1) and similarly to follow him in imitating Christ (1 Corinthians 11:1), shouldn't we be leaving behind our worries about beauty, fashion and 'outward appearance', to be replaced by an effort to become like Jesus in our characters? (Perhaps Philippians 3:7 is relevant here?) If the cost of this is Christians as a group being thought to be unfashionable, you could argue that that is not the greatest hardship we have ever faced. Should our church communities be doing much more to disprove Germaine Greer's assertion that 'Every woman knows that, regardless of all her achievements, she is a failure if she is not beautiful' (*The Whole Woman*, Anchor Books, 2000)?

The sociologist John Berger believes that 'Men act and women appear. Men look at women. Women watch themselves being looked at. This determines not only most relations between men and women, but also the relationship of women to themselves.' (*Ways of Seeing*, Penguin Books Ltd, 1990) Is it any different within the Christian community?

Should our church communities be doing much more to disprove Germaine Greer's assertion that 'Every woman knows that, regardless of all her achievements, she is a failure if she is not beautiful'

6 FALLEN BEAUTY

From a biblical perspective, the first three chapters of Genesis tell us what the Creator wanted, giving us the biblical story of human origins (not to mention the origins of everything else). The story goes that God created everything – including human beings in his own image – and it was good. But then it very quickly all went bad when human beings disobeyed God by eating forbidden fruit. In theological circles this fall from utopia is known as, well, 'The Fall'.

A common Christian understanding of Genesis 3 says that it shows three major effects of the fall on human beings: alienation from God, alienation from each other and alienation from the self (shown in Eve and Adam's shame at their own naked bodies). So, might it be possible to trace the feelings of depression, shame and guilt experienced by 70 per cent of women who were invited to spend three minutes looking at pictures of thin models, as part of a psychological study, right back to the experience of Eve, the first woman to have felt guilt and shame? In other words, if God's good creation is no longer as it should be, and we are part of that creation, why shouldn't we expect to feel that our bodies are not as they should be? Or did the fall affect only our souls and not our bodies?

... if God's good creation is no longer as it should be, and we are part of that creation, why shouldn't we expect to feel that our bodies are not as they should be? Or did the fall affect only our souls and not our bodies?

The fact that we can ask that last question shows how different our culture is from that of the first readers and hearers of the Genesis story. The entry for 'Body' in the *New Bible Dictionary (IVP, 1996)*, one of the standard biblical reference works, states that, 'The emphasis in Hebrew is not on the body as distinct from the soul or spirit. The Hebrews did not rigidly differentiate form and matter, the whole and its parts, body and soul, the body from the next self or object. The flesh body was not what partitioned a man from his neighbour, it was what bound him in the bundle of life with all men and nature'.

So, if Genesis was written with these assumptions in mind, might the writer want us to see both body and soul as affected by the fall? And could it be that the fall has affected both our bodies and our attitudes to them?

Can we take this to mean that any unease we feel about how we look shows us to be part of a broken, 'groaning' creation, desperate for release from the effects of the fall, but unsure about how to get there?

In Romans 8:18–23 Paul talks about the whole creation being 'in bondage to decay' and 'groaning' for release. Given that we're part of the created order it's perhaps not surprising that he goes on to say that we also 'groan inwardly as we wait eagerly for our adoption, the redemption of our bodies'. Can we take this to mean that any unease we feel about how we look shows us to be part of a broken, 'groaning' creation, desperate for release from the effects of the fall, but unsure about how to get there? Fat may or may not be a feminist issue, but it's certainly beginning to look like beauty and the body might be spiritual issues.

7 ETERNAL BEAUTY

... how might the idea of a 'resurrection body' change our attitude to beauty and to our present bodies?

The wider context of Paul's talk of 'groaning' in Romans 8 is the new life that Christians have 'in Christ'. This, he says, is a life and a love that not even death can separate us from. We are being transformed to be like Jesus, eventually sharing in his resurrection and also in his eternal life. But what is a Christlike take on beauty and how might the idea of a 'resurrection body' change our attitude to beauty and to our present bodies?

We don't know that much from the Gospels about Jesus' thoughts on beauty. We do know, however, that he had a definite sense of what was beautiful. He points to the lilies of the field as outshining the splendour of Solomon (Matthew 6:28,29). He makes no argument with his disciples when they remark on the beauty of the stones used in the building of the temple (Luke 21:5,6). He appreciates the beauty of the whitewashed tombs of his day (Matthew 23:27). And he describes a woman's pouring out of expensive perfume on his feet as a 'beautiful thing' (Mark 14:6). If Jesus showed a sense of what was beautiful then presumably he also possessed a sense of what was not. Is it significant, though, that not one of these Gospel references relates to a person's physical beauty? Do the Gospels show us a Jesus who is able to appreciate beauty but is so completely unconcerned with people's physical appearance that the subject is never on his lips? Is it possible for us to imagine someone like that?

Do the Gospels show us a Jesus who is able to appreciate beauty but is so completely unconcerned with people's physical appearance that the subject is never on his lips?

It's worth mentioning here that the Gospels also tell us nothing about Jesus' own physical appearance. Maybe the Gospel writers were so convinced that what mattered to Jesus was holiness of character (rather than physical appearance) that they thought it best not to mention what he actually looked like? Perhaps. And it is easy to imagine that if we knew what Jesus looked like, we might be strongly tempted to substitute being like him for looking like him. But doesn't our belief that Jesus shows us God become man – the only perfect man ever to have lived – beg the question, 'Did Jesus embody physical perfection?' If we're honest we don't give much thought to what Jesus looked like. But can you imagine Jesus being physically unattractive, either in facial features or in physique? Is there room in your heart for an ugly Jesus? Or does the very association of the words 'unattractive' and 'ugly' with the name of Jesus sound like heresy to you, even when it's got nothing to do with his character?

What makes all this even more interesting is that an Old Testament passage almost universally taken to be a prophecy about Jesus says, 'He had no beauty or majesty to attract us to him, nothing in his appearance that we should desire him' (Isaiah 53:2). Can we say, then, that from a biblical perspective you don't have to be beautiful to be perfect? And does the fact that Jesus' resurrection body still bore the marks of crucifixion (John 20:27) suggest that we could spend all eternity not looking what we would currently think of as our best?

This is a real question for us because, as was said a moment ago, Paul teaches in the New Testament that Christians will one day share in Christ's resurrection. We will have a resurrection body! This probably isn't news to you. But have you ever wondered what that body will look like? Have you always subconsciously assumed that it will conform perfectly to your perception of beauty or physical perfection? What size do you imagine you'll be in the kingdom of heaven?

Paul had rather a lot to say to the Christians at Corinth about the resurrection. A key passage is chapter 15 of his first letter to them. Before we get to that, it might

But doesn't our belief that Jesus shows us God become man – the only perfect man ever to have lived – beg the question, 'Did Jesus embody physical perfection?'

And does the fact that Jesus' resurrection body still bore the marks of crucifixion (John 20:27) suggest that we could spend all eternity not looking what we would currently think of as our best?

What size do you imagine you'll be in the kingdom of heaven?

help to know a bit about Corinth and its people.

Corinth had been a Roman colony for about a century by the time Paul arrived in AD 50. It was a city of wealth and rich culture. The citizens of Corinth worshipped many gods. Pagan belief in the immortality of the soul and the corruption of the body led them to preach and practice a sensually indulgent lifestyle. They argued that, if the body was only going to perish anyway, then why should you not be able do whatever you wanted with it while you could? These ideas were reflected in the attitudes of the church to whom 1 Corinthians 15 is addressed.

Paul uses the fact of Christ's resurrection to argue against the pagan belief that there is no resurrection. He argues that all Christian belief would be insane if Christ wasn't raised from the dead (vs 12–19). Interestingly, he then takes the Corinthians back to the story of the fall, arguing that Christ reverses its effects, bringing new resurrection life where Adam's sin brought death (1 Corinthians 15:20–23). His point seems to be that just as we all share in Adam's sin, so we can all share in Christ's resurrection life. And then he addresses the issue of the resurrection body. This, he says, has a different kind of splendour to our earthly bodies, is imperishable, glorious, powerful and spiritual (1 Corinthians 15:35–44). The change from earthly to resurrection body will happen '… in a flash, in the twinkling of an eye, at the last trumpet. For the trumpet will sound, the dead will be raised imperishable, and we will all be changed. For the perishable must clothe itself with the imperishable, and the mortal with immortality …' (1 Corinthians 15:52,53).

... how does our treatment of our earthly bodies affect the appearance of our resurrection bodies?

We can't know, of course, how that process of transformation from natural atoms into spiritual atoms will take place, but the fact that we know it is going to happen confronts us with a profound question: how does our treatment of our earthly bodies affect the appearance of our resurrection bodies? Jesus, after all, was apparently able to be recognised in his resurrection body which still bore the marks of his crucifixion. We're very familiar with the idea of our being transformed into the likeness of Christ in terms of our character, but could that process of transformation also have implications for our bodies?

BEAUTY AND DISCIPLESHIP

So, what are we to make of all of these different perspectives on what the Bible may or may not have to say about beauty? We've only scratched the surface, of course, and we've raised many more questions than we've answered. Ultimately it is in the way we live that we shall answer these questions and showcase what we believe to be a biblical approach to beauty. There are, as will be obvious from this booklet, always going to be tensions in working out what it means to live biblically, but isn't true discipleship about learning to wrestle with those tensions, rather than deny their existence?

... isn't true discipleship about learning to wrestle with those tensions, rather than deny their existence?